Creating Unique Websites
with Blogger

Clarence Galapon

ISBN 978-0-557-06645-2

Printed and bound in the United States of America

To **Emily**, John Alfred, and Lily Clare

...my everyday inspirations.

Contents

Introduction

This "Creating Unique Websites with Blogger" book offers an easy way for anyone (within reason) to get started with blogging through Google's Blogger and making his/her Blogger website truly a unique, personalized, and professional-looking website.

The objective of this book is to help you get started with Google's Blogger...and then to help you transform your Blogger website's "look and feel" from the "*I've seen a similar looking blog website like this before*" website to a website that is totally unique and yours.

This book is also helpful to people who do not necessarily want to blog, but want to have a website to showcase something. For example:
1) A person who is trying to sell/rent-out his/her house – a website of the house might help.
2) A small business owner who wants to get the word out about his/her business but does not have the budget to hire a professional web developer.
3) Everyone else who wants to have his/her own unique website that he/she can design and dynamically update without the help of a professional web developer.

What you will create

You will create five (5) unique Blogger websites! Start with a basic Blogger website, and then later on, transform it into a Blogger website that is unique on the internet.

The image below is the "after transformation" screen shot of one of the five (5) Blogger websites that you will create!

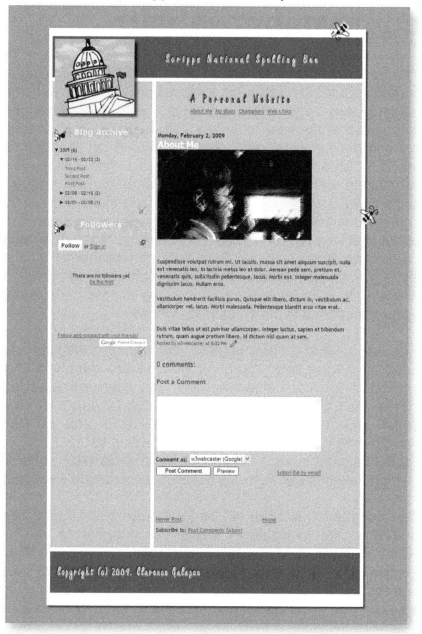

The Transformed Personal Website http://s-p-e-l-l-i-n-g-b-e-e.blogspot.com

About this book and its companion website

This book was designed with ease of reading and learning in mind … there are plenty of screenshots. It starts with the fundamentals and then proceeds with the advanced techniques in the latter chapters. However, the author does not end the fun at the end of this book! He points out – as the next step – that the reader should visit this book's companion website. This companion website makes sense since there is whole lot more of information that could not be contained within this book's 121 pages. This book then is a portal to a very dynamic body of knowledge that is available in its companion website. This book is just the "tip of the iceberg", so to speak, but your purchase of it is a prerequisite in order for you to have the access code to the secured sections of the companion website.

You can find this book's companion website at http://www.w3webcast.com/blogger/ . In the members-only section of the companion website, you may download the codes used in this book. You can then copy and paste the codes accordingly instead of typing these in. You will also find (among other things): 1) Latest updates to this book; 2) Useful tips and tricks; 3) Free and commercial backgrounds; 4) Blog covering this book; 5) Some more example websites!

This companion website will be kept current and fresh. The author will be available to answer your questions via the "Q&A" post (or other posts for that matter) within the Blog section. The Blog section of the companion website was created using Blogger! How the Blog section was created is also covered in the companion website.

Useful tools

Adobe Fireworks

Adobe Fireworks

Adobe Fireworks was used to create the static header image (among other things). It is a great tool to apply lighting and shadow effects on images. For your web images, use a resolution that is set to 72 pixels per inch (A.K.A. dots per inch (dpi)). This is the resolution that we are going to use through out this book.

Adobe Flash

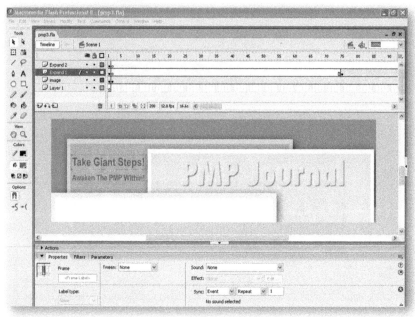

Adobe Flash

Adobe Flash was used to create the animated header for one of our example websites, PMP Journal (http://www.pmpjournal.blogspot.com).

Adobe Photoshop

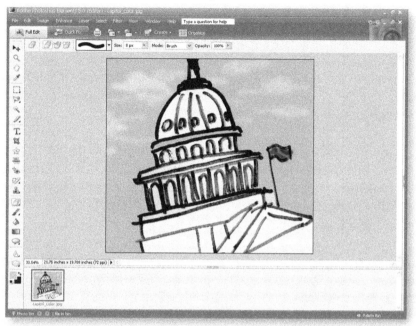

Adobe Photoshop

Adobe Photoshop was used to prepare the images for the web. For example: save the image to a size that is optimized for the web (i.e. instead of 1 Megabyte-sized image, Photoshop can make the size of the image to be saved as an image with a size of 70 kilobytes). Use this tool also to crop images and other image manipulations (i.e. coloring – like the picture that is shown here). For your web images, use a resolution that is set to 72 pixels per inch (A.K.A. dots per inch (dpi)). This is the resolution that we are going to use through out this book.

The next Steps

In a nutshell, we will do the following: 1) Create a *Spelling Bee* personal Blogger website using Google's Blogger; 2) We will then transform this template-created Blogger website into something that is unique, personalized, and professional-looking Blogger website.

Today, there are plenty of similar-looking Blogger websites on the internet – more often than not, people got the desire to have their respective template-based Blogger websites be unique, personalized, and professional. This book will help them fulfill that desire in a fun and easy manner.

The latter part of this book takes the reader to a section that shows more sophisticated approaches to transforming a basic Blogger website. Unlike the first exercise -- wherein the subject Blogger website was created from start to finish -- a ready-made Blogger website will be dissected to reveal the techniques used. You will then have to create your own Blogger websites based on what you have learned from each of the five (5) example Blogger websites. Learning is maximized by doing!

Create your basic Blogger website

Google's Blogger is one of the best and most popular blogging systems in the world. It is free, easy to setup and fun to use!

First of all you must have an email account. In this tutorial, it is already assumed that you have a Gmail email account. If you do not have a Gmail email account, get one now. Refer to Appendix "A" on how to get your own Gmail account.

When you are ready, let's get started!

Create a blog

Refer to the image below. The numbers on the image correspond to the steps below:

1) Type https://www.blogger.com into your web browser's web address box.
2) Enter your Gmail email address and password.
3) Click the "SIGN IN" button.
4) If you opt to use your own non-Gmail email account; then forget step#2 and click the "CREATE A BLOG" button...this will lead you to different screen to sign you up.

Create a blog

Sign up for Blogger

Refer to the image below. The number on the image corresponds to the step below:

1) Complete the "SIGN UP" page, and then click the "CONTINUE" button to continue

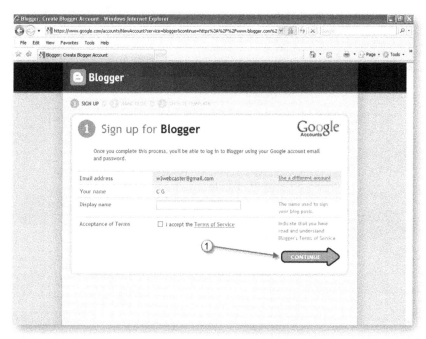

Sign up for Blogger

Name your blog

Refer to the image below. The number on the image corresponds to the step below:

1) Complete the "NAME BLOG" page, and then click the "CONTINUE" button to continue

Name your blog

Choose a template

Refer to the image below. The number on the image corresponds to the step below:

1) Choose a template (In this tutorial, scroll to the bottom and pick the "Sand Dollar" template. Of course, outside this tutorial, you may pick any template you want), and then click the "CONTINUE" button to continue

Choose a template

5

Your blog has been created!

Refer to the image below. The number on the image corresponds to the step below:

1) Congratulations! You have just created your basic Blogger website! Click the "START BLOGGING" button to start blogging!

Your blog has been created!

Blogging with your basic Blogger website

Once you have created your basic Blogger website, you may immediately start composing and posting your blogs.

Start Blogging

If you have clicked the "START BLOGGING" button after you have created your new Blogger website, the image below is what you would have seen.

Start blogging

The Dashboard

However, you may also start blogging by: 1) Opening a web browser and typing https://www.blogger.com into your browser's web address box (then pressing enter); and then, 2) Sign in with your Gmail email account with your password. Upon successful sign-in, you should see the figure below.

The Dashboard

If you click the "Edit Post", it will take you to a screen similar to the screen that is shown on the next page.

9

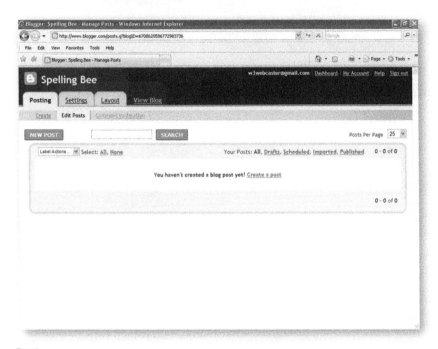

Posting

Creating, Editing, Posting

Creating, editing, and posting are self explanatory...set aside some time for you to explore these features.

When you are ready to see your website, click the "View Blog" link, it will take you to your Blogger Website.

Of course, you may also see your website by opening a new web browser and typing in the web address of your blogger website into your web browser's web address box.

The basic Blogger website

The basic Blogger website

Try entering a few blog entries to have a feel of the whole thing. Refer to the section, "**HOW TO TEST THE "LOOK AND FEEL" OF A WEBSITE USING FAKE POSTS**" (p. 36), to see how to do this the smart and quick way!

Now, we are ready to transform this basic Blogger website into a truly unique, personalized, and professional-looking Blogger website!

Transform your basic Blogger website

In this chapter, we will transform this basic Blogger website into a unique, personalized, and professional-looking website.

The figure in the next page is the "before transformation" screen shot of the website. Notice that several blog entries had been entered to give the website some substance and feel to it.

Refer to the earlier section, "**WHAT YOU WILL CREATE**" (p. VI), if you want to see the "after transformation" screen shot of the website that we are creating. The transformed website's web address is:
http://s-p-e-l-l-i-n-g-b-e-e.blogspot.com

The "Before Transformation" website

Personalize the Header

Transforming the header is always a good place to start – it immediately transforms the page in a big and dramatic way.

Step 1: You need to determine or set the dimension (width and height) of your personal header graphics. You can tell by looking at the HTML code of the Blogger website within the "Edit HTML" submenu via the "Customize" menu.

Customize

To start customizing, click on the customize link. The screen below will appear. Click on the "Edit HTML" link

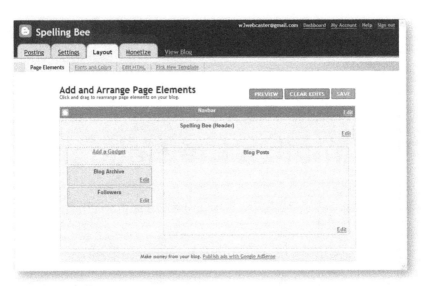

Layout -> Edit HTML

The figure below shows the HTML code that we need to customize. Scroll down until you see the code as shown. Note that the there is no width (dimension) that's specified in the "#outer-wrapper" section; hence the website takes the whole width of the screen. What we need is not for the website to take up all the width on the screen; hence we need to set the width to 800px and make sure that the webpage is located on the center. Therefore, make the "#outer-wrapper" section code looks like so (the highlight in yellow represents added code):

> #outer-wrapper {
>   font:$bodyfont;
>   width: 800px;
>   margin: 0 auto;
> }

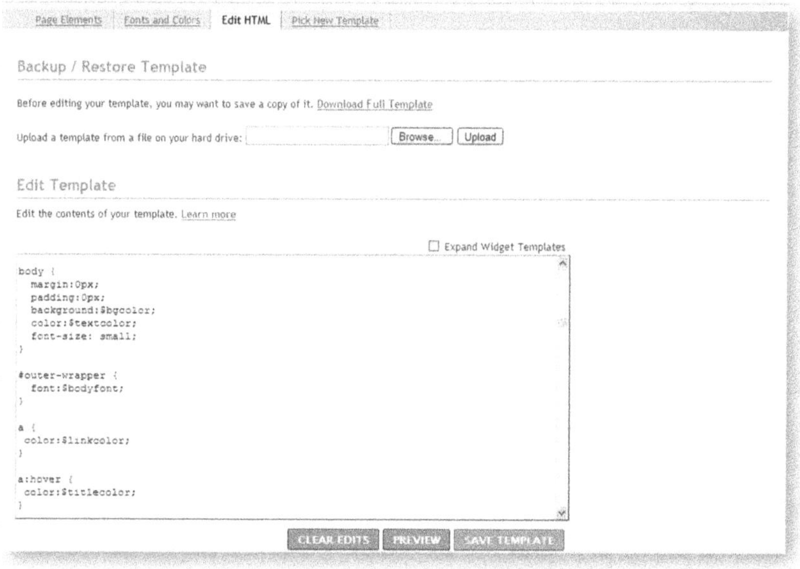

Edit HTML – set the width and location (center) of the website

Click the "SAVE TEMPLATE" and click the "View Blog" to view the revised website. The image on the next page shows how the revised website looks like.

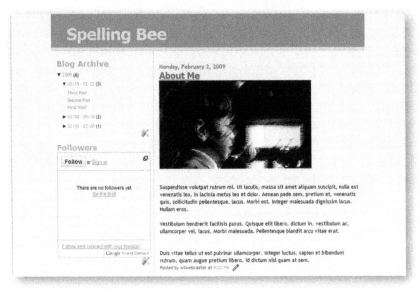

Width set and Location centered

The header graphics that we need to create then is 800px in width and the height can be 270px. You may upload this graphics (or any other images you will use in your website) to your own website or you may use Photobucket.com (www.photobucket.com) to store your graphics/images.

Go ahead and secure/produce your own header graphics/image. Once you have your own header image (and uploaded somewhere), proceed to step# 2. Remember: for your web images, use a resolution that is set to 72 pixels per inch.

Step 2: Replace the template's header image with your own header image.

Go back to the "Layout" tab and click on the "Page Elements" submenu. You should see the desired image on the next page.

16

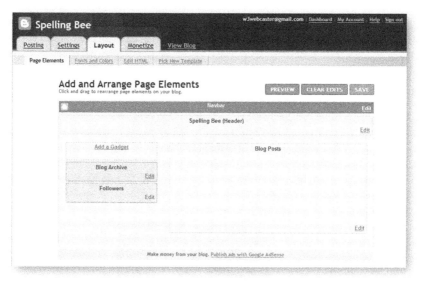

Layout -> Page Elements

Click the "Edit" link on the Header container box.

The "Configure Header" window will appear. Assign here the image that you want to be shown on the header...it could come from your computer or from the web (internet). Next is the image placement: select "Instead of title and description". Click the "SAVE" button when you are done.

Configure Header

17

Click the "View Blog" to view the revised website. The image below shows how it looks like with the personalized header.

The Personalized Header

Customize the body background

Changing the body background brings in huge additional visual positive impact.

Go back to the "Layout" tab and click on the "Edit HTML" submenu. Scroll all the way down until you find the section "*#outer-wrapper*". You should see the desired image on the next page. Try using **CRTL + F** to find; the search box will appear at the top section of the screen.

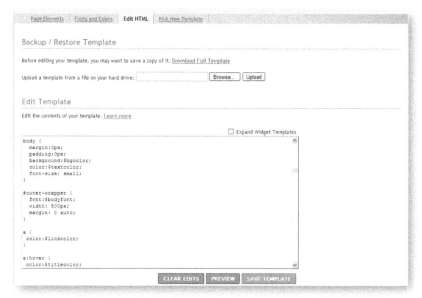

Layout -> Edit HTML

Make the "#*outer-wrapper*" section code looks like so (the highlight in yellow represents added code):

#outer-wrapper {
  font:$bodyfont;
  width: 800px;
  margin: 0 auto;
background: url(http://i617.photobucket.com/albums/tt253/cgalapon1/body_bee3.gif) top center repeat-y;
}

Make sure that you use your own background image's URL address.

Click the "SAVE TEMPLATE" button. Click the "View Blog" to review the revised website. The image on the next page shows how the revised website looks like.

Personalized Body Background

Add the Footer

Adding the footer is easy. All you have to do is add the code (refer to the code below) within the "Edit HTML" section ...paste it just after the "*</div></div> <!-- end outer-wrapper -->*" code line (scroll all the way down just above the "*</body>*" code line).

```
<div id='footer-wrapper'>
<img src='http://i617.photobucket.com/albums/tt253/cgalapon1/spelling_bee10-footer.gif'/>
</div>
```

Add the following code just above the "
/** Tweaks for layout editor preview */" code line.

```
#footer-wrapper {
  width: 800px;
  margin: 0 auto;
}
```

Click the "SAVE TEMPLATE" button and then click the "View Blog" button to view the revised website. The image below shows how the revised website looks like.

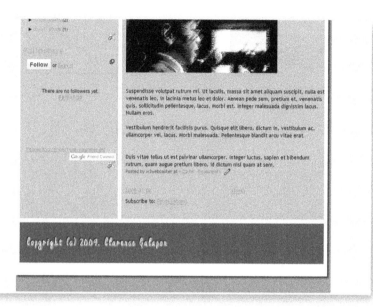

Personalized Footer

Revise page background color

In the "Edit HTML" section, find the following code:

```
<Variable name="bgcolor" description="Page Background Color"
    type="color" default="#f6f6f6" value="#f6f6f6">
```

Replace the code "*value="#f6f6f6""*" with "*value="#8794A5"*". The resulting code set should look like this:

```
<Variable name="bgcolor" description="Page Background Color"
    type="color" default="#f6f6f6" value="#8794A5">
```

Click the "SAVE TEMPLATE" button and then click the "View Blog" button to view the revised website.

The image below shows how the revised website looks like.

Revised Page Background Color

Note: You may remove the borders that you see on the main section and below the header section by:
1) Removing this code line from the *div#main* section:
   border-$startSide:dotted 1px $bordercolor;

2) Removing this code line from the *#header* section:
   border-bottom:dotted 1px $bordercolor;

The following two images illustrate the "before transformation" view and the "after transformation" full-height view of the website.

Transform your basic Blogger website

The "before transformation" website

Creating Unique Websites with Blogger

The "after transformation" Website

In essence, the transformation is complete. The rest of customizations are nice to have "add-ons" such as:

1) Fonts and Colors Customization
2) Side Bar Customization
3) Menu System
4) Making it not so ordinary by
   a. Adding page decorations using Cascading Style Sheets techniques (i.e. Bees crossing the page borders)
   b. Removing the Blogger navigation bar

Also, we will cover:

1) How to show one blog-post per page
2) How to add pictures within a blog
3) How to add videos within a blog
4) How to test the website's "look and feel" using fake posts
5) How to add, configure, rearrange, or remove Widgets
6) How to add Google's Analytics to your website

These "add-ons" and "how-to" items are now discussed.

Customize Fonts and Colors

The font color needs some adjustment for easier reading. The font style is okay; however, feel free to change the font. Click the "Customize" -> "Layout" -> "Fonts and Colors" links...this will take us to the where we can change colors and fonts of some elements within the website.

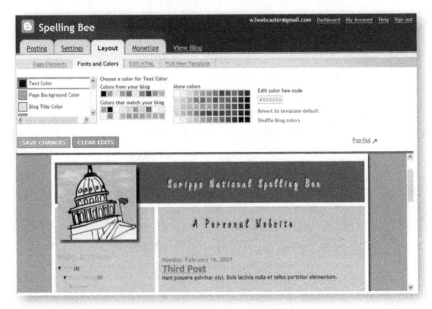

Fonts and Colors

Experiment with the colors and fonts. For this exercise, we will modify the following elements via the "Fonts and Colors" section or via the "Edit HTML" section:

Page Background Color: new value = #8794A5

Post Title Color: new value = #ffffff

Date Header Color: new value = #191919

Link Color: new value = #4c4c4c

Post Footer Link Color: new value = #333333

Visited Link Color: new value = #000000

Sidebar Title Color: new value = #f5e39e

Sidebar Link Color: new value = #191919

The resulting image is shown below

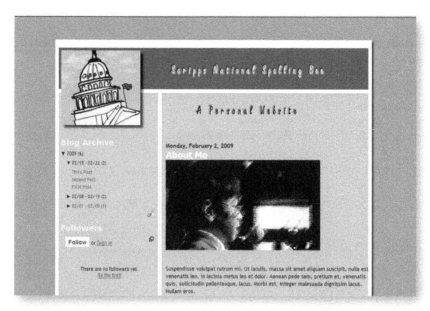

After applying the "Fonts and Colors" new settings

Side Bar Customization

The Side Bar is another great element to customize…it is easy to forget to customize this and it is also one of the most frequently used elements in the website…so customizing this element is worthwhile.

1) Go to "Customize" -> "Layout" -> "Edit HTML"
2) Locate the section "#sidebar h2"
3) Add the following codes (highlighted) like so:

```
#sidebar h2 {
 color:$sidebarcolor;
 margin:0px;
 padding:0px;
 font:$headerfont;
 background: url(http://i617.photobucket.com/albums/tt253/cgalapon1/sidebar.gif) bottom;
 height: 40px;
 text-align: center;
}
```

Click "SAVE TEMPLATE" and then click "View Blog" to review the revised website. The image below shows how the revised website looks like...notice the following items:
1) Images of "bees" on the side bar
2) The side bar height is set to 40px to fully show the graphics behind it.
3) The side bar text is centered

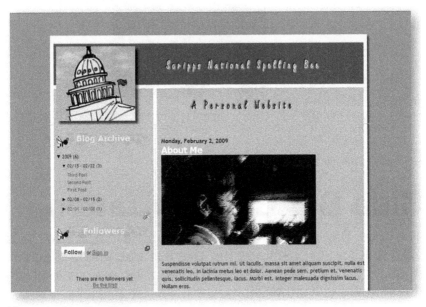

After customizing the side bar

Add a Menu System

Having a menu system on a blog site makes it more like a website. Besides, having a quick link to main parts of the blog site is very helpful. These are the menu items that we will incorporate into the website (will be located just under the "A Personal Website" sub-header:

About Me -- About the blogger

My Blogs – The blogs section

Champions – List of past Spelling Bee champions

Web Links –List of useful Spelling Bee links

First step: Create the target pages (i.e. "About Me", "Champions", and "Web Links"). No need to create the "My Blogs" due to the fact that it will display the last posted blog on the screen by just by calling out the base website address.

Create a new post titled 'About Me" to create the "About Me" target page. Click the "Post options" link and make the "Post date and time" the oldest date and time in you list of blogs to make it not the first one that comes up when entering this website.

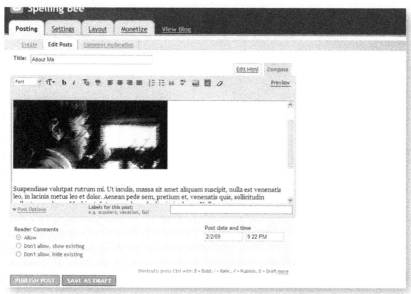

The "About me" blog entry

Click the "PUBLISH POST" button, and then click the "View Blog" link to view the revised website.

Click the newly created "About Me" blog link (not the "About Me" widget) and once the "About Me" page comes up, take note of its web page address...we will use it as the target web address of the "About Me" menu item.

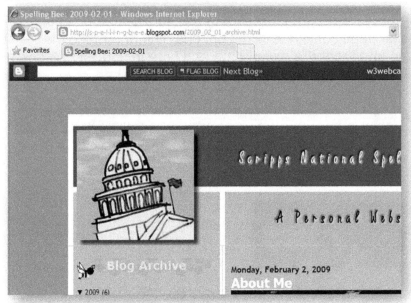

The web address of the "About me" page

Proceed and create your own "Champions" and "Web Links" pages. Make sure you write down each pages' web page address.

Also, enter about three ordinary blogs – do this after you have created the "Champions" and "Web Links" blogs.

Second step: In the HTML editor, construct the menu items.

We need two sets of code added on the HTML editor:
1) The CSS code
2) The Menu code

Add the CSS code: As usual, go to the HTML editor (via "Customize" -> "Layout" -> "Edit HTML") and add the following code just above the" /** Tweaks for layout editor preview */" code-line.

```css
#header-menu {
        position: relative;
        top: -30px;
        float: right;
        left: -185px;
}

#header-menu ul {
    list-style-type: none;
}

#header-menu ul li {
    float: left;
    margin-right: 8px;

}

#menu_div {
    height: 0px;
    width: 0px;
    float: left;
}
```

Add the Menu code: add the following code just above the "<div id='content-wrapper'>" code-line.

```html
<div class='menu_div'>
 <div id='header-menu'>
  <ul>
    <li><a href='http://s-p-e-l-l-i-n-g-b-e-e.blogspot.com/2009/02/about-me.html'>About Me</a></li>
     <li><a href='http://s-p-e-l-l-i-n-g-b-e-e.blogspot.com'>My Blogs</a></li>
     <li><a href='http://s-p-e-l-l-i-n-g-b-e-e.blogspot.com/2009/02/champions.html'>Champions</a></li>
      <li><a href='http://s-p-e-l-l-i-n-g-b-e-e.blogspot.com/2009/02/web-links.html'>Web Links</a></li>
   </ul>
  </div>
 </div>
```

Click the "SAVE TEMPLATE" button, and then click the "View Blog" link to view the revised website.

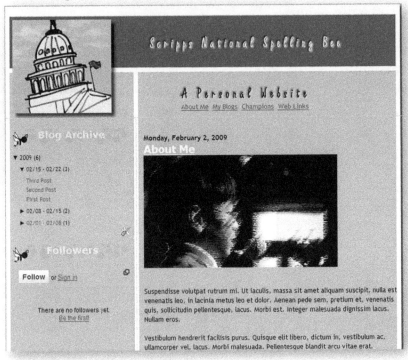

The Menu System

Making it not so Blogger-looking

There are tricks that you can use to make your website appear slicker and like it is not Blogger's:

1) Remove the Navigation Bar. Make this as the last act that you will do at the end of your website development – before you release your website to the world.

2) Add Cascading Style Sheet (CSS) Magic: Place images across page borders – it will be like "breath of fresh air" to a boring structured-looking web page.

Remove the Blogger Navigation Bar

Paste the code below just above the "/** *Tweaks for layout editor preview* */" code-line.

#navbar-iframe { display: none !important;}

Click the "SAVE TEMPLATE" button, and then click the "View Blog" to view the revised website.

Blogger's Navigation Bar removed

Since the Blogger Navigation is gone, use the "back" button to get back to the Layout editor. If you cannot get back to the

Layout editor this way, bring up a new browser…login… and you should see (upon successful login) a screen with options…one of the options is "Layout"….click this and it will take you to the Layout editor. This process is very tedious; hence make the removal of Blogger's "navigation bar" your last act before releasing the "final cut" of your website to the world.

However, there is one thing that you can do: you may comment this code line by enclosing this with "/*" at the start and "*/" at the end of this code line like so:

```
/* #navbar-iframe {   display: none !important;} */
```

This way, you do not have to delete the code line.

Add Cascading Style Sheet Magic

Add a fine touch of magic to the pages…add an image that crosses the boundaries of a given web structure. In this tutorial, we put two bees on the right and top sides of the web page. We need to add the CSS code (refer to the code below) just on top of the *"/** Tweaks for layout editor preview */"* code-line.

```
.bees {
        position: relative;
        top: 192px;
        right: 40px;
}

.bees_top {
        position: relative;
        top: -330px;
        right: 120px;
}

.bees_div {
     height: 0px;
     width: 0px;
     float: right;

}
```

To complete the code, we need to add the following code just above the "*<div class='menu_div'>*" code line:

```
<div class='bees_div'>
    <img class='bees'
src='http://i617.photobucket.com/albums/tt253/cgalapon1/bee3.png'/>
        <img class='bees_top'
src='http://i617.photobucket.com/albums/tt253/cgalapon1/bee4.png'/>
    </div>
```

Click the "SAVE TEMPLATE" button, and then click the "View Blog" button to view the revised and final website!

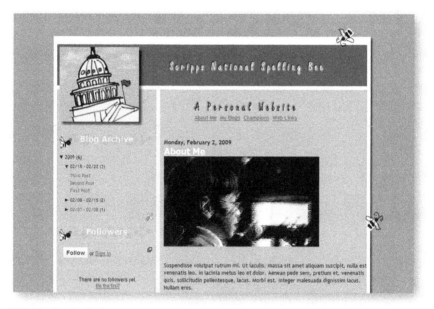

CSS Magic with the bees

How to test the "Look and Feel" of a website using fake posts

It is a good practice to test the "look and Feel" of a website with multiple posts or contents already in it during its development…that way, you can pretty much gauge how it will look like when it is fully functioning with a lot of posts (by using fake postings). If desired, you may revise the "Fonts and Colors" accordingly. Once your are happy with the "look and Feel" of your website with fake blogs, the "test posts" can then be deleted or retained just until before your first real post.

Use "Lorem Ipsum …" for the text for all three fake posts. Lorem Ipsum site is at http://www.lipsum.com/ . Use this site to generate a word, sentence(s), or paragraph(s) of which you will copy and paste into your fake blogs.

First fake post: Click the "New Post" link. If you have removed the Navigation Bar already, you may create or edit a post by logging into www.Blogger.com and log in…the go to the Dashboard…then click either the "New Post" or "Edit Posts" link.

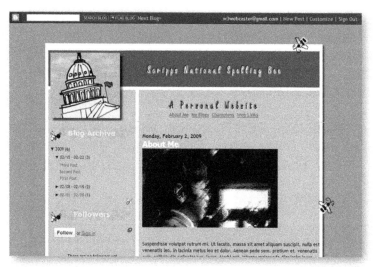

Creating a blog – New Post

Copy (from the Lorem Ipsum site) and paste the "Lorem Ipsum" text into your blog. Make sure you put text on the Title and well as on the body of the post.

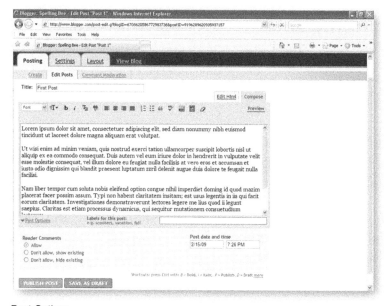

Post Options

Click the "Post Options" link to show what options you may have such as:
1) Labels for this post
2) Whether you allow or don't allow readers to comment
3) The post date and time

Click the "PUBLISH POST" button when you are done composing your Blog entry. Click "View Blog" to view changes in full. The image below shows how the first post looks like:

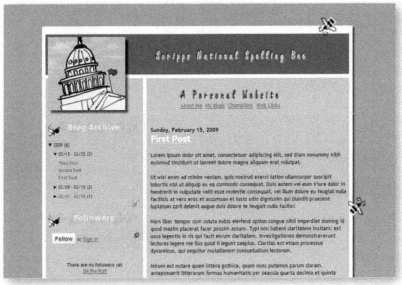

First Post – plan text

Second fake post: This time around, we will insert a picture into the post.

Click the "New Post" link. Enter "Second Post" into the Title box. Paste the "Lorem Ipsum…" text. Inserting a picture into a blog is straight-forward:

1) Position your cursor to where you want to place your picture, then click the "Add Image" button

The "Add Image" button (icon on left) within the "Posting" tab

2) The "Upload Images" window pops-up. You can either add a picture from your computer or from the web (i.e. from www.photobucket.com). You can also choose a layout and the size of the picture. Click the "UPLOAD IMAGE" button when you are done. That's it!

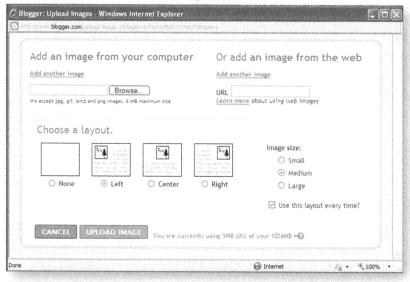

The "Upload Images" window

Click "PUBLISH POST" and click "View Blog" to view your published post. The image below shows the second post:

39

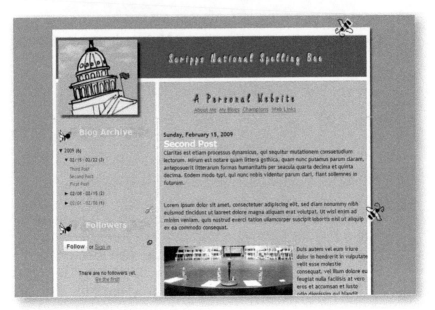

The Second Post – blog with picture

Third fake post: This post will have a video in it. My personal choice is to host my High-Definition (HD) videos on Vimeo (http://www.vimeo.com) and embed the link to it into my blog. Here is how you do it:

1) Create a new post and enter the text or story you want to share.

2) Click the "Edit Html" link.

3) Position the cursor to where you want to embed the video.

4) Copy the "Embed Code" from Vimeo and paste it within your post. For the embedded code for videos, make sure you wrap it with "<div>" at the start of the embedded code and "</div>" at the end of the embedded code…otherwise the post will not show the "Comments" section at the end of the post.

5) Click the "Compose" link.

Once you are happy with it, you click the "PUBLISH POST" and click the "View Blog" to view your new post. The next screenshot shows the new post.

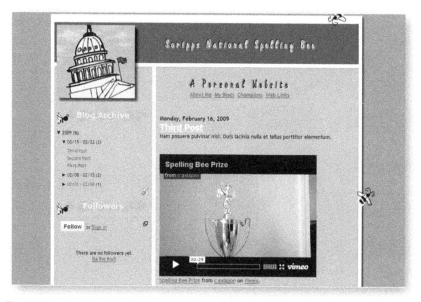

The third post -- blog with video

Show One Post at a Time

Sometimes, one would like to see one post per page...and the rest of the posts will be available under the "Blog Archive" section or Menu system of the website. To do this, 1) go to "Customize" section; 2) Click on the "Settings" tab; 3) Click on the "Formatting" link; 4) Set the value of the "Show" attribute to "1". In this tutorial, we will only show one post per page. Scroll down and click "SAVE SETTINGS", and then click the "View Blog" to view the revised website.

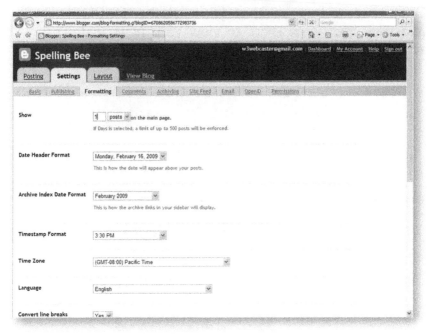

Settings – show one post on the main page

Remove, Configure, Add or Rearrange Widgets

Remove the "About Me" widget

Go to the Layout editor and click the "Edit" link within the "About Me" widget box.

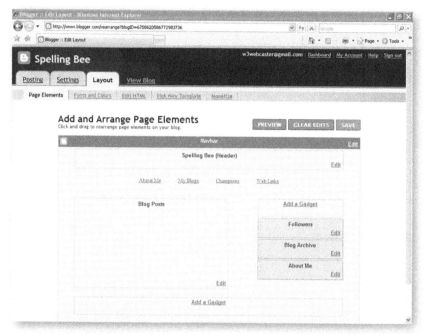

"Layout" -> "About Me -> Edit"

The "Edit Profile" window pops-up. Click the "REMOVE" button. This will remove the "About Me" widget and then takes you back to the Layout editor screen. Click the "View Blog" link to view the revised website.

Configure the "Blog Archive" widget

What we want is to set the frequency of the archiving of the blog pages to weekly (the default is monthly).

Click the "Edit" link within the "Blog Archive" widget box.

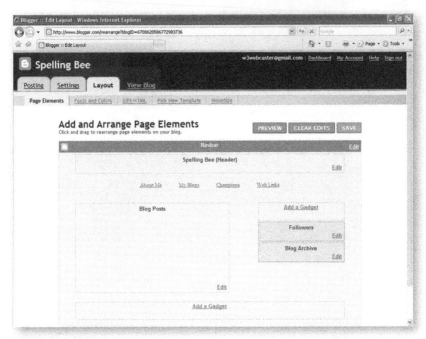

"Layout" -> "Blog Archive -> Edit"

Set the "Blog Archive" widget with the following settings:
Archive Frequency: Weekly

Configure Blog Archive Widget

Click the "SAVE" button, and then, once you are back to the Layout editor, click on the "View Blog" link to show the revised website.

Add Spelling Bee Widget

Go back to the "Layout" editor. Click the "Add a Gadget" link within the "Add a Gadget" widget box. A window will appear where in it presents you a list of available gadgets.

Type in the words "spelling bee" on the "search for gadgets" box; and then click on the "search" icon. A search result set will appear.

Pick any gadget you prefer. For this tutorial, for simplicity, let's pick the one listed at the top by clicking the "+" (add) sign. This should take you back to the "Configure Gadget" screen.

Click the "SAVE" button, and then, once you are back to the Layout editor, click the "View Blog" link to view the revised website.

Rearrange Widgets

The widgets can be rearranged within the layout. One is, however, constrained by the style of the given layout.

In this tutorial, we will put the "Followers" widget below the "Blog Archive" widget. You can do this by dragging the "Followers" widget box under the "Blog Archive" widget box.

Click the "SAVE" button, and then click the "View Blog" link to view the revised website.

Test with other Browsers

It is a good practice to test a website while it is being developed/created/revised using various web browsers to make sure the code behind it works as expected on each browser brand. For this purpose, we will use:

1) Microsoft Internet explorer
2) Google Chrome
3) Mozilla Firefox

The following screen shots reveal that our code works on all three browsers.

Microsoft Internet Explorer

Transform your basic Blogger website

Google Chrome

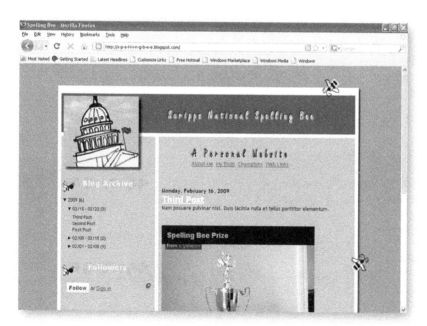

Mozilla Firefox

Add Website Analytics

Google Analytics

Do you want to know how your Blogger website is performing (i.e. how many unique and total website visitors per day, where these visitors are geographically located, etc.)? You can have these questions answered plus more by adding Google's Analytics into your Blogger website! Adding Google's web Analytics is easy. Refer to Appendix B on how to setup and use Google Analytics.

In this tutorial, once you have the "New Tracking Code" code block from Google Analytics, go to the "Edit HTML" section and paste the Google Analytics code-block immediately before the *"</body>"* code tag.

Click the "SAVE TEMPLATE" button, and then click "View Blog" to view the revised website. No visual change will show on the screen, however, the website will start "gathering information" form every website visit ready for Google Analytics to pick up for analysis later.

Sitemeter

Adding Sitemeter (www.sitemeter.com) analytics into your Blogger website is easy.

Refer to this web address link for a demo on how Sitemeter works:
http://www.sitemeter.com/flash/basic_account/basic_account.html

Advanced Techniques

Samples of customized Blogger sites that were created by the author with notation on how these were made...and along the way, techniques will be revealed.

Real Estate Website

Are you a property seller, a landlord, or a real estate owner who wants to use the internet to promote or showcase your property? Then this section is for you! This website was created using Google's blogger but it does not show as such...it shows like a professionally made unique website...and not looking like one of those Google Blogger templates that are readily available on the Internet. The techniques used to making a very unique and professional website like this are now revealed.

But first, take a look at the real estate website at:
http://realestatemarketuptowncharlotte.blogspot.com/

The figure below also shows how it looks like (with the gray page background included).

Real Estate website

The overall look

Header image, body image, footer image, and page background complete the overall look – use the technique used in the "Spelling Bee" website to put these three items together.

Template used:

Sand Dollar

Header image (width: 800px; height: 245px)

http://i617.photobucket.com/albums/tt253/cgalapon1/1805-header6-1.png

Edit the Header widget to use the Header image.

Body background image (width: 800; height: 10px)

http://i617.photobucket.com/albums/tt253/cgalapon1/1805-bg.png

This is the code…set the outer-wrapper to 800px as well:

```
#outer-wrapper {
  font:$bodyfont;
  width: 800px;
  margin: 0 auto;
    background: url(http://i617.photobucket.com/albums/tt253/cgalapon1/1805-bg.png) bottom;
}
```

Footer Image (width: 800 px; height: 245px)
http://i617.photobucket.com/albums/tt253/cgalapon1/1805-footer.png

This is the code (located just above the </body> code – scroll through the HTML code…all the way down!):

```
<div style="width: 800px; margin: 0 auto;" >
```

```
<img src='http://i617.photobucket.com/albums/tt253/cgalapon1/1805-
footer.png'/>
</div>
```

Page Background
Use color...no image needed. Go to "Fonts and Colors" section and change the "Page Background Color" value to *#8794A5*.

The menu system
The image below shows (close up) how the menu system looks like:

The Menu system

Three-widget Menu: This menu set consists of three widgets:
1) The picture is contained inside a "HTML/JavaScript" widget.
2) The main menu is contained inside a "Link List" widget
3) The "Contact Information" is contained inside a "Text" widget.

The final wireframe is shown below:

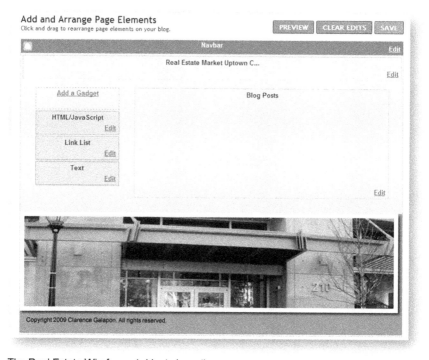

The Real Estate Wireframe (widgets layout)

The code behind the "HTML/JavaScript" widget:

```
<a href="http://i617.photobucket.com/albums/tt253/cgalapon1/kitchen2.jpg"
target="_blank"><img style="float:left; margin:0 0px 0px 0;cursor:pointer;
cursor:hand;width: 170px; height: 110px;"
src="http://i617.photobucket.com/albums/tt253/cgalapon1/kitchen2.jpg"/></a>
```

The "Link List" widget is where you set up the various menu items (each item points to a post). For example: The "New Site URL" contains the web address of the post; the "New Site Name" is the title of the post. The completed Link List is shown below:

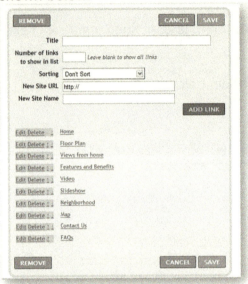

The **Link List** widget

The resulting menu has a muted white color…so change the font color to a bright white… the code is:

```
#sidebar a:link  {
 color:#ffffff
 text-decoration:none;
}
```

We want also to make the menu item highlighted as the mouse hovers over it. The code is:

```
#sidebar a:hover {
        color: #036C8A;
        background-color: #DBDBDB;

}
```

The "Text" widget is a rich text. It allows you to format the text without coding…it even creates the "mailto:" code. The code is:

```
<strong><span style="color:#000000;">Contact Information</span></strong>
email: <a href="mailto:zzz@aol.com">zzz@aol.com</a>
Phone: (123)-456-7890
```

The Posts

The posts are tweaked a bit to be able to show "Flash" contents, tables, external websites (Google maps and neighborhood websites), slideshows, and videos. These are typical website contents of a "For sale" or "For rent" property.

Home post

The first image is a "Flash" movie that pans from left to right and back…showing various pictures put together as a panorama. The "Flash" file (.swf) is contained within an Inline frame (iframe). The code used is:

```
<iframe name="Iframe1" src="http://www.w3webcast.com/1805-pan.swf"
style="float:left; margin:10px 10px 10px 0px; width: 300px; height: 199px"
scrolling="no" frameborder="no">Your browser does not support inline frames or
is currently configured not to display inline frames.</iframe>
```

Make the post date of this post to be the latest amongst the other posts – this way, this post is the first one to appear on every website visit…making this post as the home page of the website.

The second and third images are "Flash" movies that show various pictures (slide show style). This time, the image is set on the right side. This is achieved by using the code "float: right;" The code for the second image is:

```
<iframe name="Iframe2" src="http://www.w3webcast.com/1805/small_pic1.swf"
style="float:right; margin:10px 0px 10px 10px; width: 250px; height: 167px"
scrolling="no" frameborder="no">
   Your browser does not support inline frames or is currently configured not to
display inline frames.</iframe>
```

The third image used same technique…but this time, the image is on the left…the code to use is "float:left;"…like so:

```
<iframe name="Iframe3" src="http://www.w3webcast.com/1805/small_pic2.swf"
style="float:left; margin:10px 10px 10px 0px; width: 250px; height: 167px"
scrolling="no" frameborder="no">
    Your browser does not support inline frames or is currently configured not to
display inline frames.</iframe>
```

Floor Plan post and the Features and Benefits post
These posts use two-column tables to show the information – Floor plan, descriptions, photos, etc. Feel free to use CSS code instead of a table.

```
A basic table (two columns) code is this:
<table>
<tr>
<td>Insert Column 1 content here</td>
<td>Insert Column 2 content here </td>
</tr>
</table>
```

You can use this as a "Post Template" if you use tables a lot. The "Post Template" can be found at "Settings -> Formatting"

The CSS code in action may be found in one of the examples: Small Business Website. Basically using an unordered list – remember to set the column width in the #comics-menu ul li section:

```
<style>
#comics-menu {
        float: right;
}

#comics-menu ul {
    list-style-type: none;
}

#comics-menu ul li {
    float: left;
    width: 80px;  /* the column width */
    margin-right: 8px;

}
```

```
</style>


<div id='comics-menu'>
 <ul>
    <li>Put your Column 1 content here </li>
    <li>Put your Column 2 content here </li>
 </ul>
</div>
```

Views from home post

This is picture insertions with the use of "float:left" and "float: right" CSS code. This "float:right/left" technique wraps the texts around the pictures -- a nice look to the page as a whole.

Video post

This post has an embedded code – this code is generated by Vimeo. The embedded code is:

```
<object width="400" height="300"><param name="allowfullscreen" value="true"
/><param name="allowscriptaccess" value="always" /><param name="movie"
value="http://vimeo.com/moogaloop.swf?clip_id=2262283&amp;server=vimeo.co
m&amp;show_title=1&amp;show_byline=1&amp;show_portrait=0&amp;color=&a
mp;fullscreen=1" /><embed
src="http://vimeo.com/moogaloop.swf?clip_id=2262283&amp;server=vimeo.com
&amp;show_portrait=0&amp;color=&amp;fullscreen=1" type="application/x-
shockwave-flash" allowfullscreen="true" allowscriptaccess="always" width="400"
height="300"></embed></object>
```

Neighborhood post

This post used an iFrame to show an external website. The code is:

```
<iframe name="Iframe1" src="http://www.avenueuptown.com/Neighborhood.htm"
style="width: 565px; height: 366px">
   Your browser does not support inline frames or is currently configured not to
display inline frames.
   </iframe>
```

Map post

This post has an embedded code...this code is generated by Google maps. The code is:

```
<div class="right_pane" style="height: 393px">
<iframe width="560" height="350" frameborder="0" scrolling="no"
marginheight="0" marginwidth="0"
src="http://maps.google.com/maps?f=q&amp;hl=en&amp;geocode=&amp;q=210
+N.+Church+Street,+Charlotte,+N.C.+28202&amp;sll=37.0625,-
```

```
95.677068&amp;sspn=36.589577,56.25&amp;ie=UTF8&amp;g=210+N.+Church
+Street,+Charlotte,+N.C.+28202&amp;layer=c&amp;cbll=35.229041,-
80.842857&amp;panoid=jr8vERUasop-zILaB3BsWg&amp;ll=35.23931,-
80.83869&amp;spn=0.034559,0.053558&amp;z=14&amp;output=embed&amp;s
=AARTsJrTHqXVh112RzN8cllypE90HLARLA"></iframe><br /><small><a
href="http://maps.google.com/maps?f=q&amp;hl=en&amp;geocode=&amp;q=21
0+N.+Church+Street,+Charlotte,+N.C.+28202&amp;sll=37.0625,-
95.677068&amp;sspn=36.589577,56.25&amp;ie=UTF8&amp;g=210+N.+Church
+Street,+Charlotte,+N.C.+28202&amp;layer=c&amp;cbll=35.229041,-
80.842857&amp;panoid=jr8vERUasop-zILaB3BsWg&amp;ll=35.23931,-
80.83869&amp;spn=0.034559,0.053558&amp;z=14&amp;source=embed"
style="color:#0000FF;text-align:left">View Larger Map</a></small>
</div>
```

Contact Us and Frequently Asked Questions posts

These are just ordinary posts. The idea is to have a place for the reader to post some comments regarding some contact information or any other questions.

Configure Blog Posts Widget

We want to show only one post per page. To do this, configure the Blog Posts widget. Set the "Number of posts on main page" to 1. Check and uncheck the rest according to your liking. The final Blog post configuration of this website is shown below:

The **Configure Bog Post**s widget

Action Required

The best way to really learn something is through action. The same way applies to this endeavor. So, follow these next steps: 1) Download the "210Avenue.xml" template from this book's support website; 2) Upload it into a blank Blog site; 3) Familiarize yourself with the uploaded code and those that were mentioned in this book; 4) Create your own unique website based on what you have learned.

PMP Journal Website

This is a PMP website with useful posts. Features the "Search this site" search button. Features Flash as header.

Before we proceed further, take a look at the website at:

59

http://www.pmpjournal.blogspot.com

The figure below also shows how it looks like (with the gray page background included).

PMP Journal website

The overall look
Header image, body image, footer image, and page background complete the overall.

Template used
Mr. Moto Rising

Header image (A Flash movie with the following specifications: width: 828px; height: 216px). The code used is:

```
<iframe frameborder='no' name='Iframe1' scrolling='no'
src='http://www.w3webcast.com/pmp3.swf' style='width: 828px; height: 216px'>
    Your browser does not support inline frames or is currently configured not to
display inline frames.</iframe>
```

Note that you may upload your Flash movies in your own web space (if you do not have one, buy one from www.godaddy.com, for example) or use the professional version of www.photobucket.com to store your .swf (Flash files/movies) – this is not free. In this example, the author used his own web space.

Outer wrapper background image (width: 828; height: 18px)

http://i617.photobucket.com/albums/tt253/cgalapon1/body5.png

This is the code... set the outer-wrapper to 828px as well:

```
#outer-wrapper {
  margin: 0 auto;
  border: 0;
  width: 828px;
  text-align: $startSide;
  background: #8794A5
url(http://i617.photobucket.com/albums/tt253/cgalapon1/body5.png) top
$endSide repeat-y;
  font: $bodyFont;
}
```

Footer Image (width: 828px; height: 245px)
http://i617.photobucket.com/albums/tt253/cgalapon1/footer.png

This is the code (located just above the </body> code – scroll through the HTML code... all the way down!):

```
<div style='width: 828px; margin: 0 auto;'>
  <img src='http://i617.photobucket.com/albums/tt253/cgalapon1/footer.png'/>
</div>
```

Body Background
Set the body background color value to *#8794A5* via this code:

```
body {
  margin: 0;
  padding: 0;
  border: 0;
  text-align: center;
  color: $mainTextColor;
  background: #8794A5;
  font-size: small;
}
```

Special Features
This website features the following characteristics:
1) Internal web search widget
2) Top 5 posts
3) A link to the Home page
4) Revised Archive widget -- No title and states the word "Archive" as the default value
5) RSS Feed widget
6) The sidebar has changed:
   a. The Title has a yellow highlight
   b. The Items are with numbers and a light-green highlight when the mouse hovers over each item.

The techniques used in these features are now explained:

Internal web search widget
This is a Google custom search engine. You can get the code for this from http://www.google.com/coop/cse/ . Just follow the instructions. What you will end up with is one or two sets of code to embed in your website (the first set will be embedded on the spot where you want your search text and button be placed; the second set is where you want the search results be shown).

In this example, we used the "**HTML/JavaScript**" widget as the place to embed the code for the search text and search button.

Top 5 posts

The **Link List** widget is a good place to manually set the top 5 posts. This is similar to the previous example, however, this time around, it is not a menu to the whole system anymore…it is just a menu to the top 5 posts.

A link to the Home page

The Home page is the latest post…and the address is the root web address of the website. In this example, the web address is http://pmpjournal.blogspot.com/ . Use this address as the target of the link to the Home page. We used "HTML/JavaScript" widget as the place to embed the code for the link. The code is:

```
<a href="http://pmpjournal.blogspot.com/">Home</a>
```

Revised Blog Archive widget
After adding the "Archive" widget, go to the HTML code and check the checkbox for "Expand Widget Templates". Scroll down until you see this code:

```
<select expr:id='data:widget.instanceId + &quot;_ArchiveMenu&quot;'>
```

Make sure that the code under it looks like this (if not then make it so):

```
<option value="">Archive</option>
```

That is how the "Archive" word got into the dropdown box.

To get rid of the title, just click the "Edit" link on the Blog Archive widget and blank out the Title from the Configure Blog Archive window.

63

RSS Feed widget

The RSS Feed widget is one of the Basic widgets. The key to this is to know where to get the feed from. An example of a Feed URL address to input into the widget's Feed URL input box is: http://www.pmforum.org/blogs/news/rss_bn.xml

The sidebar changes

Title highlight -- here is the code:

```
.sidebar h2 {
  color: $sidebarHeaderColor;
  background-image: url(http://i617.photobucket.com/albums/tt253/cgalapon1/sb-
highlight.png);
  height: 40px;
text-align: center;
}
```

Numbered Items– here is the code:

```
.sidebar ul li {
  list-style: decimal inside;
  vertical-align: top;
  padding: 0;
  margin: 0;
}
```

The line item highlight on mouse hover – here is the code

```
.sidebar a:hover {
  color: #000000;
  background: transparent
url(http://i617.photobucket.com/albums/tt253/cgalapon1/sb-li4.png) no-repeat;
}
```

The wireframe

The image below shows the wireframe/layout of the website:

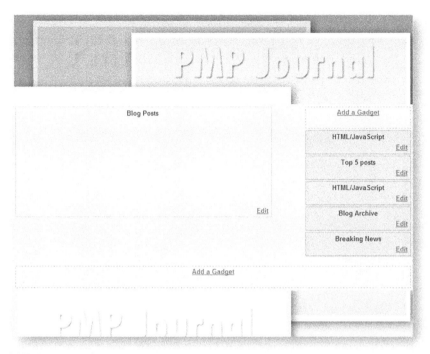

PMP Journal wireframe

Action Required

The best way to really learn something is through action. The same way applies to this endeavor. So, follow these next steps: 1) Download the "pmpjournal.xml" template from this book's support website; 2) Upload it into a blank Blog site; 3) Familiarize yourself with the uploaded code and those that were mentioned in this book; 4) Create your own unique website based on what you have learned.

Small Business Website

This is an example of a small business that sells its products online.

Before we proceed further, take a look at the website at: http://artisticyoungmind.blogspot.com/

The figure below also shows how it looks like (with the gray page background included).

Small Business website

The overall look

Header image, body image, footer image, and page background complete the overall look.

Template used

Sand Dollar

Header image (width: 936px; height: 150px)

http://i617.photobucket.com/albums/tt253/cgalapon1/artistic-header.png

Edit the Header widget to use the Header image.

Note: If the pictures from www.photobucket.com become stretchy, you might try uploading our pictures to your own web space.

Outer wrapper background image (width: 936px; height: 18px)

http://i617.photobucket.com/albums/tt253/cgalapon1/artistic-bg.png

This is the code... set the outer-wrapper to 936px as well:

```
#outer-wrapper {
  font:$bodyfont;
  width: 936px;
  margin: 0 auto;
  background:  url(http://i617.photobucket.com/albums/tt253/cgalapon1/artistic-bg.png) top center repeat-y;
}
```

Footer Image (width: 936px; height: 100px)
http://i617.photobucket.com/albums/tt253/cgalapon1/artistic-footerr.png

67

This is the code (located just above the *</body>* code – scroll through the HTML code…all the way down!):

```
<div style="width: 936px; margin: 0 auto;" >
<img src='http://i617.photobucket.com/albums/tt253/cgalapon1/artistic-
footerr.png'/>
</div>
```

Page Background

Use color…no image needed. Go to "Fonts and Colors" section and change the "Page Background Color" value to #607078.

Special Features

This website features the following characteristics:
1) Flash movie embedded in a post
2) Use of table to format a post
3) Use of Link List widget for creating a menu
4) Use of Adobe Fireworks to collage a clickable image
5) Use of Pay Pal to sell an item
6) Use of CSS to show the details of an item on mouse hover. For example: A simple list of items to sell (with Image) and a bigger image pops-up when the mouse hovers over it
7) Use of CSS to format a post like a table would
8) Use of CSS to switch between a "black and white" image to a "color" image on mouse hover

The techniques used in these special features are now explained

Flash

The use of Flash is rampant in this website. Flash was used to 1) Display details of an image; 2) To not have the user the ability to save the image into their local space (via "right-click ->save as " for example) – since the images are copyrighted materials.

Home page: The "Home" page is the latest post. Make sure that this "Home" page is the latest post (amongst the other posts in this blog) all the time.

The Flash movie code (embedded at the top-most portion of the post) is shown below:

```
<iframe name="Iframe1" src="http://www.w3webcast.com/harvest-pan600.swf"
style="width: 600px; height: 300px" scrolling="no" frameborder="no">
   Your browser does not support inline frames or is currently configured not to
display inline frames.</iframe>
```

Table to format a Post

Just below the Flash movie is a two-column, one-row table. The first column houses the "Latest News"; whereas the second column houses the facts about the image that is shown in the Flash movie. The second column also houses a picture in a Flash (.swf) format for piracy protection. The code is:

```
<table style="width: 600px; float: left; text-align: left; vertical-align: top"
align="left">
<tr>
<td style="vertical-align: top;">
Column 1, Place the Latest News here.</td>
<td style="vertical-align: top;" >
<iframe name="Iframe1" src="http://www.w3webcast.com/harvest-600-430.swf"
style="float:left; margin:10px 10px 10px 10px;width: 300px; height: 215px"
scrolling="no" frameborder="no">
   Your browser does not support inline frames or is currently configured not to
display inline frames.</iframe>
Place Column 2 text here</td>
</tr>
</table>
```

This technique (use a table) is also used in the "News and events post".

Link List for a Menu

This is the same technique that was used in previous examples. Please check those out for more details.

Clickable Image

You can place web links on several places on an image (Adobe Fireworks created image) – these are also called hotspots. So, when the user clicks on the hotspot, a web browser will open up with the web address that is associated to that hotspot. This technique was used in the Paintings post. When the user clicks on one of the art images, a bigger picture of the art will be shown in another post. From there, the user may purchase that particular art via Pay Pal.

Pay Pal

The code for a one item purchase with Pay Pal is the easiest to setup (compared to the other options from Pay Pal). Check out www.paypal.com for details. For the examples used in this website, the Harvest post for example, the code for the "Buy now using Pay pal" link is:

```
<a href="https://www.paypal.com/cgi-
bin/webscr?cmd=_xclick&business=herschelgomez@xyzzyu.com&item_name=H
arvest&item_number=harvest1&amount=0%2e01&currency_code=USD">Buy
now using Paypal</a>
```

You have to customize the above-mentioned code with the details of your PayPal business (get this from www.paypal.com), the name of your product, your product number, and your product checkout price.

Simple List with Image and Pop-up Image on mouse hover

One nice thing to do is to present the user with a list of items for sale with a small picture version beside it. The user may then put his/her mouse over the small picture to see the bigger picture and the opportunity to buy via Pay Pal. This technique was used in the Drawing gallery post.

The trick to this technique is two folds. 1) Use a CSS code for each item (Regular settings: to define the size of the image, the name of the image. On mouse hover: to define the size of the bigger image, the name of the bigger image); 2) Attach the CCS code id to the link on the post.

Here is an example of the CSS code:

```
<!-- Drawings Gallery css. one style per drawing: start -->
<style type='text/css'>
a.d1 {
display: block;
width: 200px;
height: 152px;
background: transparent url(http://www.w3webcast.com/themazeofthelostsmall-
copyr.jpg) no-repeat;
}

a.d1:hover {
display: block;
width: 620px;
height: 620px;
background: transparent url(http://www.w3webcast.com/themazeofthelost-
text.png) no-repeat;
}
</style>
```

Here is the example of the post that used the CSS code id= d1.

```
<a class="d1" href="https://www.paypal.com/cgi-
bin/webscr?cmd=_xclick&business=herschelgomez@xyzzyu.com&item_name=T
heMazeOfTheLost&item_number=TheMazeOfTheLost01&amount=0%2e01&curr
ency_code=USD"></a>The Maze of the Lost
</br>
```

Use of CSS to format a post

You may borrow the technique that was used to create a menu for this purpose. The Comics gallery post used this technique. There are two code sets: 1) The CSS code; 2) The post code.

The CSS code is:

```
#comics-menu {
        float: right;
}

#comics-menu ul {
list-style-type: none;
```

```
}
#comics-menu ul li {
float: left;
margin-right: 8px;

}
```

The post is (uses the CSS code):

```
<div id='comics-menu'>
  <ul>
    <li>Item 1</li>
    <li>Item 2</li>
  </ul>
</div>
```

You may set boundaries (i.e. set the width of the comics-menu to a certain px; set the width of the LI to a certain px). When the boundaries are exceeded, the line items (LI) will wrap around forming a column similar to a table.

Use of CSS to switch between a "black and white" image to a "multi-color" image on mouse hover

This technique uses a regular image (black and white) then uses a background image (multi-color) on mouse hover. This technique was used in the Comics gallery post. There are two codes: 1) The CSS code; 2) The post code.

The CSS code is:

```
<style type='text/css'>
a.c1 {
display: block;
width: 200px;
height: 152px;
background: transparent url(http://www.w3webcast.com/themazeofthelostsmall-copyr.jpg) no-repeat;
}

a.c1:hover {
display: block;
width: 200px;
height: 152px;
background: transparent url(http://www.w3webcast.com/themazeofthelostsmall-color.jpg) no-repeat;
}
</style>
```

The post code is:

```
<a class="c1" href="https://www.paypal.com/cgi-
bin/webscr?cmd=_xclick&business=herschelgomez@xyzzyu.com&item_name=T
heMazeOfTheLost&item_number=TheMazeOfTheLost01&amount=0%2e01&curr
ency_code=USD"></a>The Maze of the Lost
```

The code also goes to Pay Pal when the larger image is clicked.

The Wireframe

Here is the wireframe/layout of the website

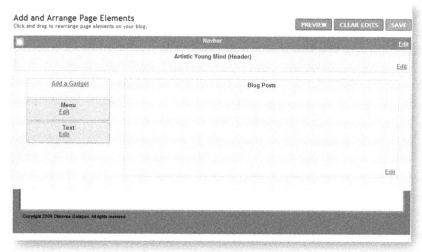

The **Artistic Young Mind** wireframe

Action Required

The best way to really learn something is through action. The same way applies to this endeavor. So, follow these next steps:1) Download the "artistic.xml" template from this book's support website; 2) Upload it into a blank Blog site; 3) Familiarize yourself with the uploaded code and those that were mentioned in this book; 4) Create your own unique website based on what you have learned.

Another version of this website is available. This version uses: 1) A fixed background image (one big image); 2) A transparent header image; 3) A transparent footer image. No need for a body image. It also uses a code to set the background as fixed and centered (just like the one used in the Windows screen...the single-picture background (not tiled)).

See the code and learn from it: The best way to follow this version is: 1) Download the "artistic2.xml" template from this book's support website; 2) Upload it into a blank Blog site; 3) Familiarize yourself with the uploaded code and those that were mentioned in this book; 4) Create your own unique website based on what you have learned.

Here is how the other version looks like:

Artistic Young Mind website version 2

The overall look

Header image, body background image, and the footer image complete the overall look.

Template used

Sand Dollar

Header image (width: 936px; height: 150px)

http://i617.photobucket.com/albums/tt253/cgalapon1/artistic2
-header.png

Edit the Header widget to use the Header image.

Note: If the pictures from www.photobucket.com become
stretchy, you might try uploading our pictures to your own
web space.

Body background image (width: 1450px; height: 1100px)

http://i617.photobucket.com/albums/tt253/cgalapon1/art-
harvest2-1450-1100.jpg

This is the code:

```
body {
  margin:0px;
  padding:0px;
  background:$bgcolor;
  color:$textcolor;
  font-size: small;
/* added this for artistic 2 start */
  background-image: url('http://i617.photobucket.com/albums/tt253/cgalapon1/art-
harvest2-1450-1100.jpg');
  background-position: center;
  background-repeat: no-repeat;
  background-attachment: fixed;
/* for artistic 2 end */
}
```

Set the outer-wrapper to 936px as well – remove any
page/body background image away from here:

```
#outer-wrapper {
  font:$bodyfont;
  width: 936px;
  margin: 0 auto;
}
```

Footer Image (width: 936px; height: 100px)
http://i617.photobucket.com/albums/tt253/cgalapon1/artistic2
-footerr-1.png

This is the code (located just above the *</body>* code –
scroll through the HTML code…all the way down!):

```
<div style='width: 936px; margin: 0 auto;'>
<img src='http://i617.photobucket.com/albums/tt253/cgalapon1/artistic2-
footerr.png'/>
</div>
```

News Website

This is a website with tons of posts in multi-column and
menu-linked Blog sites.

This example features a multi-column template with a menu
system and a search mechanism. The menu system offers a
way to put together a set of blog sites. This style is ideal
when one have tons of multi-topic news or information (from
"Politics Blog site" to "Entertainment Blog site").

But first, take a look at the website at:
http://theloremipsumpost.blogspot.com/

The figure below also shows how it looks.

THE LOREM IPSUM POST

Home Politics Media Business Finance Sports Entertainment Living Style Charlotte Comedy Video Bogger Index Archive
Bios Get Email Alerts Make this your homepage [Google Custom Search] [Search]

Joblessness Reaches 10% in
Bloomberg
Texas, North Carolina,
Illinois and Ohio rounded
out the six states with the
biggest loss of jobs.
"Economic weakness is
greatest in parts of the
country ...

Discrimination: Who is
Business Management
Daily, USA
By William Sturges William
H. Sturges is a partner in the
Charlotte, NC office of
Shumaker, Loop &
Kendrick, LLP. He is the
administrator of the
litigation ...

For high-speed rail, Georgia
Atlanta Journal
Constitution, USA
Compare that with North
Carolina, where big bucks
may end up funding
construction of actual train
lines that lead to
Washington. Georgia and
North Carolina ...

NC Domino's duo jailed for
The Palmetto Scoop, USA
... 31, were charged by
police in Conover – about
an hour northwest of
Charlotte – with
distributing prohibited
foods, a felony in North
Carolina. ...
Related Articles »

powered by Google™

Monday, April 13, 2009

Post one

Lorem ipsum dolor sit amet, consectetur adipiscing elit. Mauris sit amet lorem. Maecenas tempor velit et velit. Etiam dictum libero a nunc.

Mauris ac lorem. Integer tristique augue eu metus posuere tempor. Mauris vehicula, lacus id feugiat euismod, felis nulla dictum odio, a suscipit magna leo ac erat. Quisque sapien nibh, ornare eget, sagittis at, egestas eu, tortor. Cras ut ante sit amet diam vehicula pretium.

Morbi vestibulum dui eu nunc. Proin in tellus sed neque faucibus euismod. Fusce interdum. Sed imperdiet tincidunt odio. Donec vehicula vestibulum odio. Suspendisse at erat. Cras id diam eu sem fermentum cursus.

Phasellus molestie, nulla sit amet ultricies auctor, justo sem volutpat metus, in sodales tellus sapien sit amet neque. Mauris dui. Quisque quis est. Sed dignissim magna ut ipsum dignissim egestas.
Posted by w3gwebcaster at 12:21 PM 0 comments
Subscribe to: Posts (Atom)

Blog Archive

[Blog Archive ▼]

Did you vote for

○ Democrat
○ Republican
○ Other
○ Did not vote

[Vote] Show results

Votes so far: 0
Days left to vote: 0

Did you like the post?

○ Yes
○ No
○ Maybe
○ Did not read it

[Vote] Show results

Votes so far: 0
Days left to vote: 0

Finance

BAC CITI FNM FRE AI G

Pressure mounts on bofa
Reuters
By Martha Graybow NEW
YORK, April 17 (Reuters) -
Two influential investor
advisory groups sharply
rebuked Bank of America
Corp (BAC. ...
Related Articles »

Exxon Mobil, Bank of
Wall Street Journal
Exxon Mobil topped the list
in late trading on Friday for
Buying on Weakness, which
tracks stocks that fell in
price but had the largest
inflow of money. ...

US STOCKS SNAPSHOT-
Reuters
Standouts included
technology and financial
shares, with Bank of
America (BAC.N: Quote,
Profile, Research) up more
than 7 percent to $11.13
ahead of the ...
Related Articles »

Get Ready for Ken Lewis
thestockmasters, USA
Get ready for Bank of
America's (NYSE:BAC) Q1
Earnings call tomorrow and
the talking heads expect
them to report a profit of 5
cents a share. ...

powered by Google™

The Lorem Impsum Post website

The overall look

The adopted look for this website was meant to be plain – we will leave it to the reader to put their own Header image, body background image, and the footer image complete the overall look. Nonetheless, the plain look is nice and refreshing – no further work needed!

Template used

Minima Stretch
We took a bit of a deviation here. This template features widths in percentages…so when you resize your browser, any component (with width set to percent) will resize as well.

Of course, you may set some components to a fixed width when or if you want it.

Header image (none)
We just changed the Header title's color to green and made the font bigger.

Body background image (none)

Footer Image (none)

Width
In this example, we set the width of the whole website to 970px. This is the code:

```
#outer-wrapper {
  margin:0;
  padding:10px;
  text-align:$startSide;
  font: $bodyfont;
  width:970px;
  margin: 0 auto;
  }
```

Three columns plus two columns
So, here is how we got this template to have a three column body instead of the usual two. Once you get the idea, you may have more than three columns.

The Main idea
1) Duplicate the side bar – the duplicate will be the additional column. Make sure you give the duplicate a unique name.
2) Declare the duplicate sidebar in the <body> of the HTML code
3) Resize the components accordingly so that the width of the website (the container) remains the same but the contents' (widgets) width values are changed to fit collectively within the container's given width (total width of all widgets in one line should be 100%, spaces included; or the total width of all widgets in on

line should be equal to the total width of the website, spaces included).

The code
Duplicate the sidebar

The widget "sidebarS1-wrapper" is the duplicate (lower code set)

```
#sidebar-wrapper {
  margin-$endSide: 2%;
  width: 18%; /*from 25%*/
  float: $endSide;
  display: inline;      /* fix for doubling margin in IE */
  word-wrap: break-word; /* fix for long text breaking sidebar float in IE */
  overflow: hidden;     /* fix for long non-text content breaking IE sidebar float */
}

#sidebarS1-wrapper {
  margin-$startSide: 2%;
  width: 18%;
  float: $startSide;
  display: inline;      /* fix for doubling margin in IE */
  word-wrap: break-word; /* fix for long text breaking sidebar float in IE */
  overflow: hidden;     /* fix for long non-text content breaking IE sidebar float */
}
```

Declare the added sidebar

Since we want the new column to be shown before the "main" section (where the posts appear), we place the new column's code just before the code <div id='main-wrapper'>.

```
<div id='sidebarS1-wrapper'>
  <b:section class='sidebar' id='sidebarS1' preferred='no'>
</b:section>
  </div>

<div id='main-wrapper'>
```

Resize the following wrappers: sidebar, main, sidebarS1.
The width and spaces included.
The code

```
#sidebar-wrapper {
  margin-$endSide: 2%;
  width: 18%; /*from 25%*/
  float: $endSide;
```

80

```
   display: inline;      /* fix for doubling margin in IE */
   word-wrap: break-word; /* fix for long text breaking sidebar float in IE
   */
    overflow: hidden;      /* fix for long non-text content breaking IE
   sidebar float */
   }

   #main-wrapper {
     margin-$startSide: 2%;
     width: 52%;  /* from 67% */
     float: $startSide;
     display: inline;      /* fix for doubling margin in IE */
     word-wrap: break-word; /* fix for long text breaking sidebar float in IE
   */
      overflow: hidden;      /* fix for long non-text content breaking IE
     sidebar float */
      }

   #sidebarS1-wrapper {
     margin-$startSide: 2%;
     width: 18%;
     float: $startSide;
     display: inline;      /* fix for doubling margin in IE */
     word-wrap: break-word; /* fix for long text breaking sidebar float in IE
   */
      overflow: hidden;      /* fix for long non-text content breaking IE
     sidebar float */
     }
```

That's all there is to it!

Additional Column under the "main" section
Another thing to do to drive home the idea on how to add columns…add two columns under the "main" section.

Again, same procedure: 1) Duplicate the sidebar; 2) Declare the duplicate sidebar(s); 3) Resize components accordingly.

Duplicate the sidebars

```
   #sidebarM1-wrapper {
     margin-$endSide: 1%;
     width: 49%;
     float: $startSide;
     display: inline;      /* fix for doubling margin in IE */
     word-wrap: break-word; /* fix for long text breaking sidebar float in IE */
     overflow: hidden;      /* fix for long non-text content breaking IE sidebar float */
   }

   #sidebarM2-wrapper {
     margin-$endSide: 1%;
```

```
width: 49%;
float: $startSide;
display: inline;      /* fix for doubling margin in IE */
word-wrap: break-word; /* fix for long text breaking sidebar float in IE */
overflow: hidden;      /* fix for long non-text content breaking IE sidebar float */
)
```

Declare the sidebars

Since we want these sidebars (columns) to be under the "main" section, we have to place the code just before the closing </div> of the "main-wrapper" section. The code is:

```
<div id='sidebarM1-wrapper'>
  <b:section class='sidebar' id='sidebarM1' preferred='no'>
<b:widget id='Poll2' locked='false' title='Did you vote for' type='Poll'/>
</b:section>
  </div>

<div id='sidebarM2-wrapper'>
  <b:section class='sidebar' id='sidebarM2' preferred='no'>
<b:widget id='Poll1' locked='false' title='Did you like the post?' type='Poll'/>
</b:section>
  </div>

</div> <!--of 'main-wrapper' -->
```

Resize

Note that resize within the parameters of the main section, not the whole website width.

```
#sidebarM1-wrapper {
  margin-$endSide: 1%;
  width: 49%;
  float: $startSide;
  display: inline;      /* fix for doubling margin in IE */
  word-wrap: break-word; /* fix for long text breaking sidebar float in IE */
  overflow: hidden;      /* fix for long non-text content breaking IE sidebar float */
}

#sidebarM2-wrapper {
  margin-$endSide: 1%;
  width: 49%;
  float: $startSide;
  display: inline;      /* fix for doubling margin in IE */
  word-wrap: break-word; /* fix for long text breaking sidebar float in IE */
  overflow: hidden;      /* fix for long non-text content breaking IE sidebar float */
)
```

The Lorem Ipsum Post Wireframe

The image below shows how the Layout looks like. The footer (now floats at the top) may be switched off by removing the code (located at the bottom of the HTML code). The code to remove is:

```
<div id='footer-wrapper'>
  <b:section class='footer' id='footer'/>
</div>
```

However, you might want not to remove it so you have a place to put the "Copyright" and other usual things that go with the Footer of a website.

The Lorem Ipsum Post wireframe

The Menu to Other Blogs

The "HTML/JavaScript" widget just under the Header contains the menu code. The Menu code is found in the companion website of this book.

Three columns plus two columns revised

Another exercise is to add a one wider column (as wide as the main) under the two columns within the main section. It

83

uses an approach similar to the previous example. We leave this exercise for you, the reader, to complete. The answer is available in this book's companion website. In the companion website, you will find other examples with various column formats including a four-column template.

The following images show how the above-mentioned exercise would look like in a wireframe and in a website (a preview of the four-column website is also shown). This website is shown when you click the "Entertainment" menu item on the "The Lorem Ipsum Post" website. The web address is: http://theloremepsumpost-entertainment.blogspot.com .

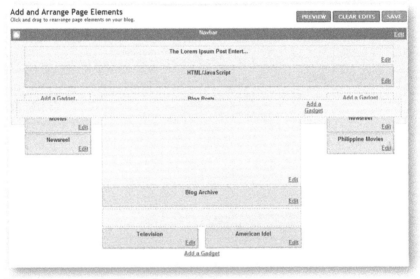

The Lorem Ipsum Post Entertainment Wireframe

THE LOREM IPSUM POST
ENTERTAINMENT

Home   Politics   Media   Business   Finance   Sports   Entertainment   Living   Style   Charlotte   Comedy   Video   Bogger Index   Archive   Bios   Get Email Alerts   Make this your homepage

[Search]

Movies

The top movies at the North
Reuters
'Hannah Montana: The Movie" was released by Walt Disney Pictures, a unit of Walt Disney Co (DIS.N).
"Crank: High Voltage" and 'The Haunting in Connecticut" ...
Related Articles »

DAILY NEWS MOVIE
New York Daily News, USA
Lanky and lank-haired Zac Efron may be the embodiment of eternally-recurring youth in his new movie, "17 Again," but if the teen heartthrobs of earlier ...
Related Articles »

Huff Post review - State of
Huffington Post, USA
It mourns the death of traditional journalism, traditional movie stars, and even traditional movies. One cannot dispute that State of Play represents a fine ...
Related Articles »

Box Office Report: Zac to
TIME
The box-office results tell us a bit about who can be counted on to go to the movies to see their favorites. Efron, carrying a movie for the first time ...
Related Articles »

powered by Google

BOXING: Golden attraction
Daily Breeze, USA
By Robert Morales, Boxing Columnist It was 3:30 pm Tuesday, about three hours after Oscar De La Hoya announced his retirement from boxing. ...
Related Articles »

Racine boxer decks all
Milwaukee Journal Sentinel, USA
Fields, representing the Racine Boxing Club, out-pointed Andre Sawyer of Twitter message several hours after he defeated his Mexican nemesis Ulises Solis in ...
Related Articles »

Olympic boxer won't face
USA Today
DURHAM, England (AP) — Olympic boxer Bradley Saunders of Britain will not face charges over a tin of cocaine found in his garden. Durham police say Friday ...
Related Articles »

powered by Google

Monday, April 13, 2009

Entertainment News Post

Lorem ipsum dolor sit amet, consectetur adipiscing elit. Mauris sit amet lorem. Maecenas tempor velit et velit. Etiam dictum libero a nunc. Mauris ac lorem. Integer tristique augue eu metus posuere tempor. Mauris vehicula, lacus id feugiat euismod, felis nulla dictum odio, a suscipit magna leo ac erat. Quisque sapien nibh, ornare eget, sagittis at, egestas eu, tortor. Cras ut ante sit amet diam vehicula pretium. Morbi vestibulum dui eu nunc. Proin in tellus sed neque faucibus euismod.

Fusce interdum. Sed imperdiet tincidunt odio. Donec vehicula vestibulum odio. Suspendisse at erat. Cras id diam eu sem fermentum cursus. Phasellus molestie, nulla sit amet ultricies auctor, justo sem volutpat metus, in sodales tellus sapien sit amet neque. Mauris dui. Quisque quis est. Sed dignissim magna ut ipsum dignissim egestas.

Pellentesque quam justo, rhoncus quis, tristique nec, sodales id, lectus. In faucibus dolor sodales tellus. Integer et ligula. Donec eu velit at magna sagittis sagittis. Quisque sit amet purus. Phasellus nunc nisl, tempus a, adipiscing eget, sollicitudin non, turpis. Cras odio. Duis pharetra nibh sed sem. Praesent euismod ligula et ipsum hendrerit venenatis. Aliquam iaculis rhoncus nisl.

Aliquam tincidunt rhoncus purus. Etiam bibendum mattis dui. Quisque et nulla. Aenean a sapien nec libero tempus ultrices. Aenean eu lectus. Nulla auctor diam vitae lorem. Pellentesque tincidunt dolor et purus. Praesent neque sapien, venenatis eget, mattis sed, adipiscing vitae, leo. Pellentesque tristique.
Posted by w3webcaster at 6:45 PM 0 comments
Subscribe to: Posts (Atom)

Blog Archive

[Blog Archive ▾]

Television

Television   actors   shows

SAG, studios reach tentative agreement
Los Angeles Times, USA
With fewer members working in television, SAG has seen a sharp falloff in income from membership dues. The loss of income combined with heavy expenditures, ...
Related Articles »

Susan Boyle is the Reason We Love
About - News & Issues, USA
The people we meet through reality television are not characters created in the minds of writers. The folks we get to know on reality television are real ...

WNGS-TV sold to Dallas religious
Buffalo News, United States
By Alan Pergament WNGS-TV, the independent station in Springville that recently switched its programming

American Idol

American Idol Results Show: Judges
Associated Content, USA
Matt Giraud has made history on American Idol when the judges saved him from getting kicked off the show after American viewers gave him the least amount of ...
Related Articles »

Failed Australian idol contestant stalks
NEWS.com.au
POLICE in California have arrested a former failed American Idol contestant caught peering through Britney Spears' windows. Miranda Tozier-Robbins was ...
Related Articles »

'American Idol' tour set to start on July
Entertainment Weekly
The top 10 contestants from this season of American Idol will hit the road for a nationwide tour starting July 5 in

Search YouTube

Dr. Oz's Free Test
Millions have already taken this amazing test. What's your RealAge?
Ads by Google

◁▷ Spiritual Fitness Tips   Zytu

Oscar de la Hoya
Newsday, USA
Sure, he lost to Manny Pacquiao, Floyd Mayweather, Bernard Hopkins, Shane Mosley twice and Felix Trinidad. A win against one or two of those fighters ...
Related Articles »

Press your pants! Why I'll
Examiner.com
I make no bones about the fact that I am rooting. I am hoping and I expect Manny Pacquiao to thrash Ricky Hatton on May 2 in Las Vegas. ...
Related Articles »

Manny Pacquiao vs. Ricky
Newsday, USA
In addition to what should be a great matchup between Manny Pacquiao and Ricky Hatton on May 2, the undercard will feature WBC super featherweight champ ...
Related Articles »

EA Sports: Pacquiao vs
Examiner.com
While the fight doesn't go down until May 2nd, EA Sports is going to give us a chance to replay the fight using Fight Night Round 4 demo. ...

powered by Google

Philippine Movies

Better late than later
Inquirer.net
I, for one, want to build up a video library of good Filipino movies, to share with friends the best fruits of the current indie film wave. ...

Working not for the money
Philippine Star, Philippines
The two actors, along with fellow cast member Amy Brenneman, met with The Philippine Star in Los Angeles recently during the

Only in Hollywood Filipino
Inquirer.net
He also worked as a musician on the score of Filipino movies. "I can't think of any word to explain the excitement we feel," shared Bob, who is the founding ...

powered by Google

The Lorem Ipsum Post Entertainment website

THE LOREM IPSUM POST
ENTERTAINMENT

Home Politics Media Business Finance Sports Entertainment Living Style Charlotte Comedy Video Bogger Index Archive
Bios Get Email Alerts Make this your homepage [Google Custom Search] [Search]

Movies

Amazon: You Bring The
ChannelWeb, USA
Now you can if you rent
movies from Amazon.com,
which Tuesday expanded its
Amazon Video on Demand
service to include high-
definition movies and TV
shows. ...
Related Articles »

Earth Day movies
San Francisco Chronicle,
USA
But if you want to end the
day with a movie, here is a
list of environmentally
themed films for the whole
family. The latest Bond film
is here, too, ...
Related Articles »

Bai Ling cranks up

Monday, April 13, 2009

Entertainment News Post

Lorem ipsum dolor sit amet, consectetur
adipiscing elit. Mauris sit amet lorem. Maecenas
tempor velit et velit. Etiam dictum libero a nunc.
Mauris ac lorem. Integer tristique augue eu metus
posuere tempor. Mauris vehicula, lacus id feugiat
euismod, felis nulla dictum odio, a suscipit magna
leo ac erat. Quisque sapien nibh, ornare eget,
sagittis at, egestas eu, tortor. Cras ut ante sit amet
diam vehicula pretium. Morbi vestibulum dui eu
nunc. Proin in tellus sed neque faucibus euismod.

Fusce interdum. Sed imperdiet tincidunt odio.
Donec vehicula vestibulum odio. Suspendisse at
erat. Cras id diam eu sem fermentum cursus.
Phasellus molestie, nulla sit amet ultricies auctor,
justo sem volutpat metus, in sodales tellus sapien
sit amet neque. Mauris dui. Quisque quis est. Sed
dignissim magna ut ipsum dignissim egestas.

Pellentesque quam justo, rhoncus quis, tristique

The Amazing Race 14: Did
BuddyTV, USA
Like what Oscar said before,
this season of The Amazing
Race has been mostly blah
for me. The difference is, I
skipped a couple of seasons
before returning ...
Related Articles »

'Amazing Race' host stops in
Iowa City Press Citizen, USA
The wind was blowing and
the temperatures were in
the low 40s when Phil
Keoghan, host of CBS's The
Amazing Race, rode into
Hubbard Park on the
University of ...
Related Articles »

Amazing Racers Talk
Seattle Post Intelligencer
By JOYCE ENG It seemed
inevitable that
stuntmen/brothers Mark

HBO's 24/7 Pacquiao-
Newsday, USA
Christian Bale, who was
born in Wales, showed up in
Pacquiao's camp. Wonder if
he's a Hatton fan? Or a Joe
Calzaghe fan? And from
what we can see, ...
Related Articles »

Hatton vs Pacquiao fight
Reuters
LOS ANGELES (Reuters) -
The IBO light-welterweight
title fight between Ricky
Hatton of Britain and
Filipino Manny Pacquiao
next week has been sold
out, ...

Christian Bale joins Mark
Entertainment Weekly
Because I'm obsessed with
HBO's great documentary
boxing series,
Pacquiao/Hatton 24/7. The

The Lorem Ipsum Post Entertainment website with four Columns

Next steps

Visit this book's companion website at
http://www.w3webcast.com/blogger/. In there, in the
members-only section in particular, you will find (among
other things): 1) Latest updates and additions to this book; 2)
Useful tips and tricks; 3) Free and commercial backgrounds;
4) Blog covering this book; 5) Some more example websites!

Your purchase of this book is your ticket to the members-
only section of the companion website. This companion
website will be kept current and fresh. The author will be
available to answer your questions via the "Q&A" post (or
other posts for that matter) within the Blog section of the
companion website.

Appendix A: Get your own Gmail email account

Gmail is a new kind of webmail, built on the idea that email can be more intuitive, efficient, and useful. And maybe even fun.

Follow the following steps to get your own Gmail email account:

Creating Unique Websites with Blogger

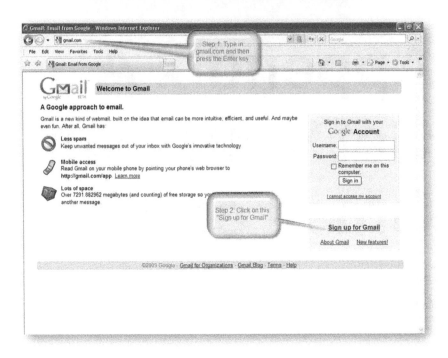

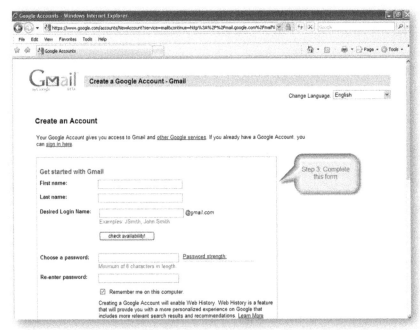

Appendix A: Get your own Gmail email account

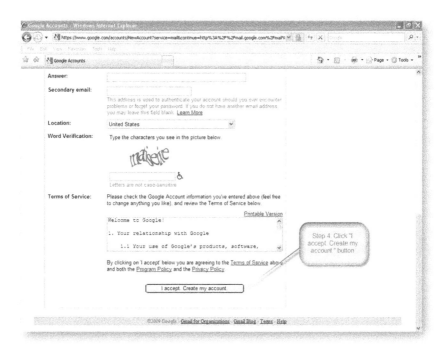

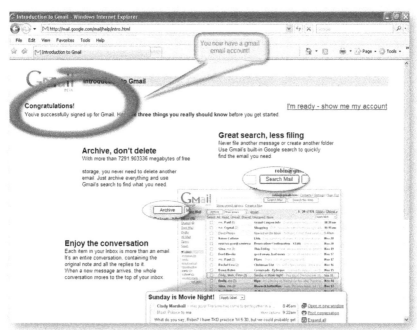

Next Steps

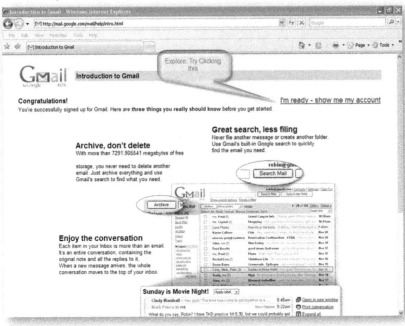

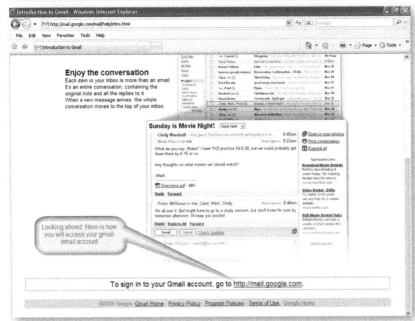

Appendix A: Get your own Gmail email account

Appendix B: Setting up and Using Google Analytics

Setting up Google Analytics

Setting up your Google Analytics is easy.

Type in http://www.google.com/analytics

Click the "Access Analytics" button to go to the Analytics sign-in page.

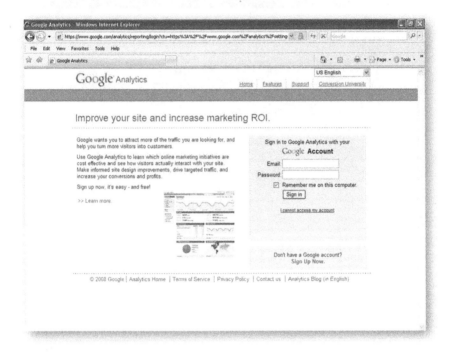

Enter your G-mail email address and your password, and then click the "Sign in" button to get to the Analytics Screen. If you do not have a Google account, click the "Sign Up Now" link.

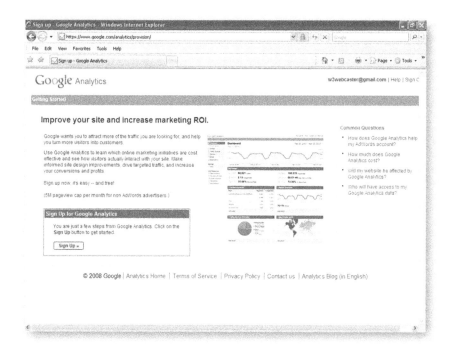

Click the "Sign Up" button. This sign-up screen only appears once – when there is no Analytics in place for your Google account. Once you have an Analytics in place, you should see a list of websites that you are tracking or analyzing.

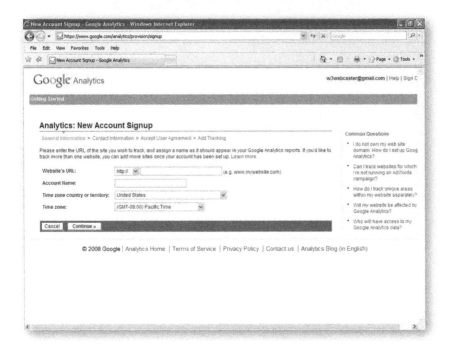

Complete this form and click the "Continue" button.

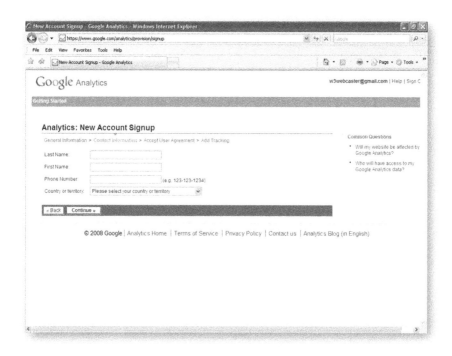

Complete this form, and then click the "Continue" button.

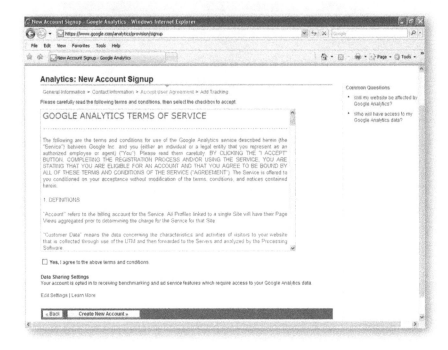

Check the checkbox, and then click the "Create New Account" button.

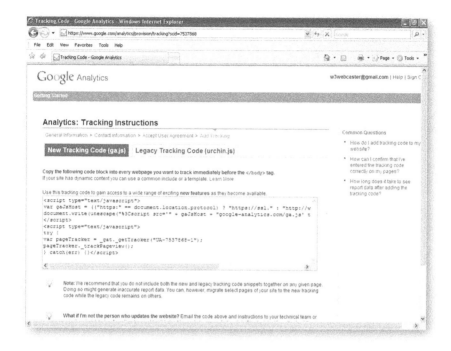

The "New Tracking Code" appears on the screen. You copy this code block into every webpage you want to track immediately before the </body> tag.

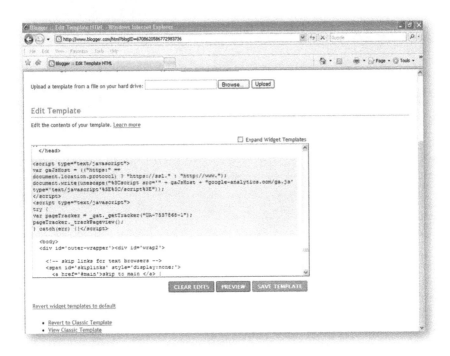

That's all there is to it for setting up a "tracking device" for Google' web analytics.

Refer back to the "New Tracking Code" screen, scroll down and click the "Continue" button. This will take you to the Analytics page of the website(s) that you are tracking.

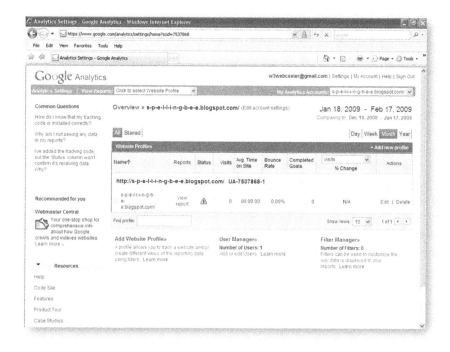

Click on the "View Report" link to see the Analytics report.

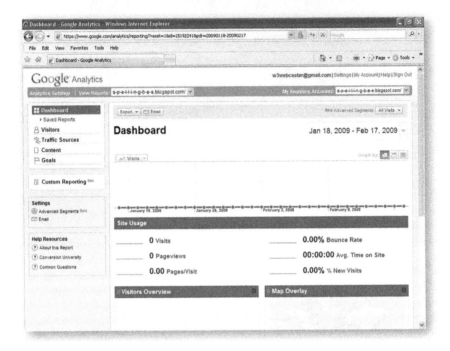

All you have to do now is to wait for web traffic and see how your website is performing.

Using Google Analytics

Using your Google Analytics is easy.

Type in http://www.google.com/analytics

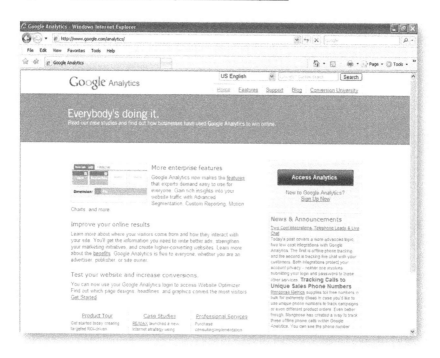

Click the "Access Analytics" button to go to the Analytics sign-in page.

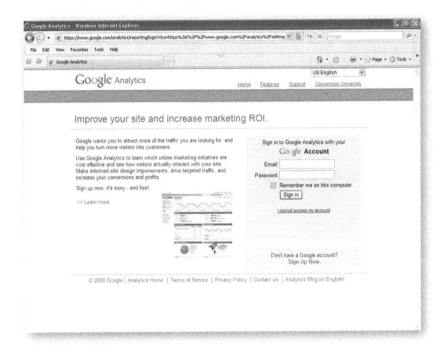

Enter your G-mail email address and your password, and then click the "Sign in" button to get to the Analytics Screen. If you do not have a Google account, click the "Sign Up Now" link.

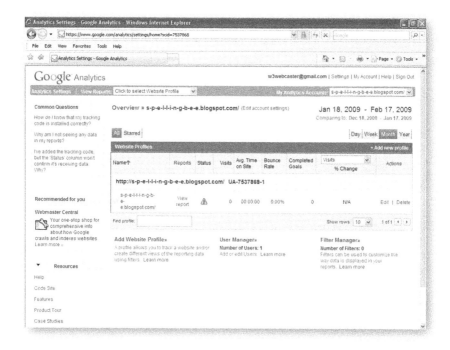

Click on the "View Report" link to see the Analytics report.

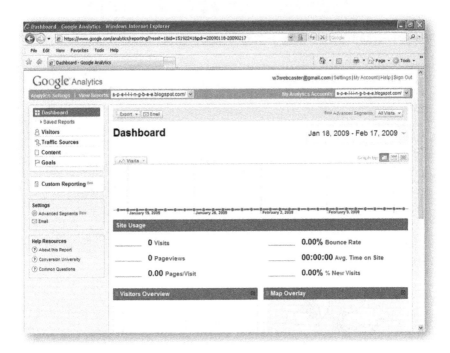

All done and congratulations! All you have to do now is to wait for web traffic and see how your website is performing.

Index